Soap Making Recipes Book 4:

Glycerin Soap Recipes

By

Angela Pierce

Table of Contents

Introduction 5
1. Glycerin Orange Oil Soap 9
2. Glycerin and Shea Butter Soap 10
3. Glycerin and Salt Soap 11
4. Glycerin Coffee Bean Soap 14
5. Glycerin Rose Soap 16
6. Glycerin Goat Milk Soap 18
7. Glycerin and Lavender Soap 20
8. Glycerin Beeswax Soap 22
9. Multi- Layered Rainbow Glycerin Soap 24
10. Glycerin Soap Base 27
11. Glycerin and Chamomile Soap 30
12. Marmalade and Glycerin Soap 32
13. Rosemary and Lavender Glycerin Soap 34
Tips for Making Glycerin Soap 36
Conclusion 38
Thank You Page 39

Soap Making Recipes Book 4: Glycerin Soap Recipes

By Angela Pierce

© Copyright 2014 Angela Pierce

Reproduction or translation of any part of this work beyond that permitted by section 107 or 108 of the 1976 United States Copyright Act without permission of the copyright owner is unlawful. Requests for permission or further information should be addressed to the author.

This publication is designed to provide accurate and authoritative information in regard to the subject matter covered. This work is sold with the understanding that the publisher is not engaged in rendering legal, accounting, or other professional services. If legal advice or other expert assistance is required, the services of a competent professional person should be sought.

First Published, 2014

Printed in the United States of America

Introduction

People use soaps religiously and happily add them in their daily hygienic routine. This ritual following can be turned into more beauty oriented experience by carefully choosing the soap containing the best content for your skin. Yes, beauty is no more the concern of women only as men equally show concern for their skin and looks. Getting the soap containing the contents you want is quite tough as they are pre pack with many contents, whether you like it or not you have to use it. But the great thing is, now you can easily make your own beauty soaps at home with ingredients of your choice, even customized it with refreshing fragrances to soothe and refresh your bathing time.

The best ingredients to add in your soap is glycerin as it has a lot of proven skin benefits, it not only add glow to your skin but also helps you keep younger for longer to fight wrinkles, so calling it an anti-wrinkle formula is not that bad. So let's explore some of its benefits for your skin as follows:

1. **Humectant:** Glycerin is a great help to retain water in your skin for longer, especially in the hot summer and dry winter when you need the water retention in your skin more. Well, it also draws water from the air into the skin and called as hygroscopic in nature.

2. **A skin treatment:** If you are worried about oily skin and struggling with pimples then the best thing to try out to get back your beautiful skin is glycerin. Yes glycerin helps to protect your skin from bacterial infections and also helps to reduce oil and protect your skin from pimples.

3. **Moisturizer:** Glycerin is a great moisturizer, especially for oily skin. You can use it by adding in it water or rose water. Do not apply directly to oily skin with diluting it and do not let it longer on your skin as its sticky nature catches a lot of dirt. So be saved and enjoy it's a lot of benefits.

4. **As Face Pack:** You love to treat your skin on daily or weekly basis with face mask or face packs then glycerin is the best thing to add in your face pack with fuller's earth. You can add in it the rose water and apply on your face and neck and enjoy the fresh and clean skin daily.

5. **Skin repairer:** Skin gets cracked and rough due to dirt and dry air. Especially when skin is low in water content. Glycerin is the best treatment to give your skin for retaining back the glow and structure. It also keeps your skin hydrated and prevent moisture loss.

6. **No Side effects:** The best thing is it do not have any side effects. It is already a main ingredient of many lotions or soaps and it is quite gentle on the skin. It is also used to treat many diseases especially skin diseases like eczema and psoriasis.

So, after knowing all these benefits I think it's the best ingredient to try a soap with. If you are wondering why it is necessary to make a soap at home as there are a lot available in the market already. Yes, there are, but if you want to have a safe, healthy and pure ingredient soap free of chemicals then it is best to get yourself one by preparing at home. Moreover, you can add fragrance of your choice and even give the soap any shape, different from the conventional round shape.

Therefore, let's get yourself some good recipes and prepare a sweet fragrance, beauty soap for you and your loved ones. It is not a bad idea to gift some homemade soaps to your family and friends this

Christmas or on their birthday. So here we go with some easy and amazing recipes.

1. Glycerin Orange Oil Soap

Ingredients:

-2 Cups of Glycerin Soap Base

- 7 drops of orange oil (sweet)

- 2 drops of colorant (orange)

- ½ cup of jewelweed maceration (boiled in ½ cup of water)

Directions:

Take the glycerin soap base and melt it down into a boiler or microwave. Once melt down completely, now add in it the Jewelweed maceration and stir them together until the base get cooled slightly. Now add the color and fragrance and mix the mixture well. Now take the mold of any size and shape and pour the soap in it and put it into a cool place to get hard and cooled down. Unmold it and enjoy your first homemade glycerin soap with amazing color and fragrance.

2. Glycerin and Shea Butter Soap

Ingredients:

-2 Cups of glycerin soap base

- 5 drops of essential oil (orange)

- 2 Tbsp. of Shea butter (melted)

- 1 mold of any shape and size

Directions:

First completely melt down the glycerin soap base in microwave or in the boiler. Then add in it the melted Shea butter and mix thoroughly when the mixture get cooled little bit, add in it the 5 drops of essential oil and mix thoroughly. Now pour the mixture into a mold and keep aside to cool down. Once cooled, unmold and enjoy the refreshing and moisturizing soap, it is best for dry skin.

3. Glycerin and Salt Soap

Don't wonder about adding salt and use of salt in soap. It will provide you a great Exfoliator and help you to cleanse your skin thoroughly. Most people love to make glycerin soaps having salt in it. But be careful while using it on your body as it has salt in it and will disturb you once touch bruises and cuts on the skin. It is recommended not to use this soap on your face or sensitive skin.

Ingredients:

-1 Pound of glycerin

-1 teaspoon essential oil (any of your choice)

- 1 teaspoon organic dye (any color)

Directions:

Take the glycerin in a bowl and melt it down in the microwave for 2 minutes without stirring. Keep the microwave on high. Now add the oil and due in the melted glycerin and stir the mixture slowly until combined together well. Be careful do not stir vigorously as it will introduce bubbles into the mixture.

Now pour the mixture into a nonstick pan and put aside for 2 hours to cool down. Once the mixture gets cooled completely, cut it down into bars.

Now follow the following instructions to add salt in it, for it you need to melt down the soap again, but before it you need to prepare following ingredients:

-1/4 cup of sea salt

- 2 teaspoons table salt

- 1 mold

Directions:

Now first add the soap into a boiler and melt it down completely. Now add in it the table salt and stir the mixture slowly and carefully. Pour the mixture into the soap mold and leave a cup still in the bowl. Do not let the mixture to get had, while it is still liquid, add in it the sea salt by sprinkling over the mixture surface and cover the whole surface of the mixture with it. Now pour the left over mixture from the bowl into the mold over the sea salt and cover it completely by carefully pouring it evenly over the surface.

Now place the mold in a cooler place and even you, can put it into a freezer for 2 hours. Once cooled down unmold the soap and cut it into bars and use when it as per requirement. Even you can keep it longer by disposing it properly in cabinet.

4. Glycerin Coffee Bean Soap

Ingredients:

-Essential Oils

- Soap Dye (any color)

- Mold

- Shea Butter

- Glycerin soap base

- Ground coffee beans

Directions:

Take soap mold and clean them properly, grease them with oil and set aside. Now take the glycerin soap and base and melt it down into the microwave. Once it gets melted completely take it off and add in it the oil, coffee bean and stir well. Do it quickly as glycerin will set up fast. Now pour this mixture into the mold and let it sit for almost an hour. Once the soap gets cooled down and hard in the mold. Carefully unmold it and let it dry in the air for a few more hours. Your soap is ready to use and to be wrapped as gift for some loved one.

5. Glycerin Rose Soap

Ingredients:

-Glycerin soap base

- 5 – 6 drops of dye or color

- Alcohol spray

- Double boiler

- Soap mold

- 4 – 5 drops of rose essential oil

- Petroleum jelly

- rose petals (just few)

Instructions:

Take glycerin soap base and melt it down in the double boiler by keeping the flame on low. While melting the glycerin soap base, set the water and rose petals to boil. Once the petals get boiled, pick them out of the water and place them on the tissue paper to dry out the remaining water from them.

Now add the dye, essential oil and rose petals into the melted glycerin base and stir well. Take the mold and apply petroleum jelly in it. Pour the mixture into the mold and set it aside for some minutes. Now spray alcohol over it and place the mold for 2 – 4 hours to cool down. Once it gets cooled unmold the soap and use as necessary.

6. Glycerin Goat Milk Soap

Ingredients:

-Rose petals (few)

- Some drops of food color or dye

- Little bit of petroleum jelly or vegetable oil

- Mold

- Glycerin soap base

- Essential oil

- Microwave

- 2 Tablespoon of goat milk powder

Instructions:

Melt down the glycerin soap base in the microwave or double boiler. One melted down completely, add in it the goat milk powder. Stir the mixture well and cook for some time on low heat, now add the dye and essential oil and mix the mixture again.

Take the soap mold and grease it with vegetable oil and pour in it the mixture carefully. Now leave it for some minutes to set in it well. Now put the mold in a cold place to let mixture cool down and get hard, it will take some hours. Once the mixture gets cool and hard, unmold the soap and wrap it into plastic paper to use and store.

7. Glycerin and Lavender Soap

Ingredients:

-1 soap bar of glycerin

- Food color or dye (purple)

- distilled water

- Soap molds

- Some Lavender flowers

- Double boiler or microwave

- Petroleum jelly

- 7 – 10 drops Lavender essential oil

Directions:

Take 1 glycerin soap base bar and melt it down into the boiler or microwave on low flame. While the glycerin bar is melting down into the boiler. Take a bowl and add in it the distilled water and some lavender flowers and keep them to boil. Let the water and flowers to boil for 2- 3 minutes. Remove the bowl from the heat and pick the flowers from the water and put on the tissue. Now add these flowers, essential oil and purple dye into the melted glycerin. Stir the mixture well until combined together completely.

Now take the soap mold and grease it with the petroleum jelly. You can take one big mold and some little molds of any shape to give your soap different look. Now pour the glycerin and other ingredients mixture into the mold carefully as it is hot and you can even burn away your hand. Now keep this mixture to settle down well into the mold.

Let the mixture to cool down for almost 3 hours. Once the mixture gets hard and cooled down completely, unmold the soap carefully and wrap it into the plastic wrapper to store and you can keep them for 2 – 4 hours in air to let them completely dry, if you want to have these soap for longer under running water. You can also store them longer if wrapped it properly in plastic paper. Enjoy the great smelling lavender soap.

8. Glycerin Beeswax Soap

Ingredients:

-1 Tbsp. of Honey

- Alcohol spray

- Vegetable oil

- 1 cup of Glycerin

- Soap mold

- Boiler

- 1 tbsp. of beeswax

- Dye or color (Yellow)

Instructions:

Take a bowl, add in it 1 cup of glycerin and melt it down in the double boiler. Now add beeswax in it and stir it well, put it on the low flame to cook down for some time. Now stir the material slowly until both glycerin and beeswax get melted down and combine together. Add honey into the mixture and keep on stirring until mix well. Now take a soap mold of your choice and grease it with a little bit of vegetable oil. Pour the mixture into the mold and keep aside for some time to settle down. Now put the mold in a cool place for almost 3 hours. Once the soap gets cooled and hard, unmold it and use as per your requirements.

9. Multi- Layered Rainbow Glycerin Soap

Ingredients:

-2 drops of dye or color (take 2 different colors)

- Petroleum jelly

- Boiler

- Soap Mold

- 10 drops of essential oil

- Alcohol for spray

- 2 bars of Glycerin Soap

Instructions:

Take the Glycerin soap bars in the container and place them in the microwave oven or boiler for 30 seconds, After 30 seconds swirl the container and keep it again for 30 seconds. Repeat the same process until all the soap get melt.

Now remove the container and divide the melted glycerin soap mixture into two separate bowl. Now add essential oil in both the mixtures and also first food color in one mixture and second food color in the other mixture. Stir the mixtures well until the color mix well and give a uniform look.

Now take the soap mold and grease it with the petroleum jelly or vegetable oil. Pour the first mixture into the mold (half of it) then spray the alcohol over it and let it little bit cool. Now take the second mixture and pour over the layer of the first mixture in the mold. Again spray with alcohol to remove air bubbles. Now again pour the remaining first mixture over the layer of second mixture in the mold. Spray it with alcohol. Every time you pour the one mixture over the other, make sure that the layer of the first mixture is little bit hard. Otherwise the both layers will get mingled and you won't get the desired result and clarity in layered structure of the soap.

Now keep the mold in a cool and airy place. You can keep it in the refrigerator too. Wait for soap to cool down completely at least 3 – 4 hours. Once the soap gets hardened completely, unmold the soap. If the mold you utilized in preparing soap was wider than you can cut the soap into little bars, for it always use sharp knife to avoid breakage and cracking of soap.

If you want to store it for longer than you can even wrap them in plastic paper and store it for later use. Your multi-layered glycerin soap is ready to go under water, it is also a great pleasing gift for kids.

10. Glycerin Soap Base

If you want to make glycerin soap base at home too then by following this easy recipe you can easily prepare it at home too, otherwise you can easy purchase it from the market.

Ingredients:

-1 pound of Coconut Oil

- 8 Ounces of Glycerin

- 2 pound and 8 ounces of Palm oil

- 1 pound and 12 ounces of ethanol

- 12 ounces of lye

- 1 pound and 9 ounces of Castor oil

- 15 ounces of distilled water (having dissolved sugar of 1 pound and 4 ounces)

- 1 pound and 9 ounces of distilled water

Instructions:

Firstly, measure the water and lye and mix them together. Never add water into the lye, always take water into a container and then slowly and gradually add lye in it and stir carefully. Now place this mixture at 135 – 145 F to cool down.

Now mix all the oil and heat them, once combine together, let them cool down until attained the same temperature as lye solution. Now gradually mix the oils into the lye and water solution and stir the both mixtures together slowly and carefully. Now add in it the alcohol and stir the mixture for 5 minutes until a clear solution is formed.

Now cover the container with the plastic covering to avoid quick evaporation of alcohol while mixture will boil. Now place this container into a large bowl containing softly boiling water. Within five minutes of the boiling the plastic will puff off and the mixture will start to boil. Adjust the temperature to keep the constant boiling temperature at low heat. It will take 2 hours to completely neutralize the mixture.

After 2 hours stir the glycerin solution and keep on stirring the solution for 3 minutes. Now test the solution by putting a spoonful of glycerin solution onto a glass, if it's clear then it's done if not then allow the solution to boil again by adding 2 ounces of alcohol in it. Once it is done let it sit for 15 minutes and then add in it the color and fragrances and stir well. Now you can pour this mixture into the mold and let it cool down by keeping in a low temperature environment for 4 – 5 hours. Unmold the soap and cut it into bars to use it for preparing colored glycerin soap.

11. Glycerin and Chamomile Soap

Ingredients:

-2 cups of glycerin soap base

- 1 tbsp. of glycerin

- 1 tbsp. of chamomile powder

- 1 capsule of chlorophyll concentrate

Directions:

Take the glycerin soap base bar and melt it down into the boiler and microwave on low flame or heat. Now take the chamomile powder and blend it with the glycerin. Now add this chamomile powder mixture into the melted glycerin mixture and stir both the mixture well until combine together properly. Also add in it the chlorophyll capsule and stir the mixture again.

Now take the soap mold and grease it with the vegetable oil and pour the mixture into the mold slowly and carefully. Let the mixture to settle down for 2- 3 minutes and spray with the rubbing alcohol to avoid formation to bubbles. Now place the mold in the cold environment to cool down for 3 – 4 hours. Once the mixture get hard and cold, unmold the soap carefully and cut it into bars. You can also store this soap for further use by wrapping it into the plastic wrapper. If you want your soap to last linger under tap then it's recommended to let it dry for 2 – 3 weeks.

12. Marmalade and Glycerin Soap

Ingredients:

-Dye or color (Orange)

- Essential Oil (for fragrance you can choose any of your choice)

- 2 ¾ cup of grated glycerin soap base bar

- A pinch of dried chamomile flowers or marigold flowers

- Soap Mold

- Vegetable oil

- Boiler or microwave

Directions to Prepare:

Take the grated glycerin soap base bar into a bowl and put it into the double boiler or microwave on low heat to melt down. Do not stir in between. Once the glycerin soap gets melted completely, add in it the orange dye and stir well. Turn off the heat and add in it essential oil and dried marigold flowers and stir the mixture well.

Now take the soap mold of any size or shape and pour the soap mixture in it and let the mixture to get set for 2- 3 minutes in the mold. Now place the mold in some cold place to cool down for 4- 5 hours. Once it get cooled, unmold the soap and cut it into bars. You can wrap it into a plastic paper to store for future use. Enjoy your beauty soap and collect appreciation from your family and friends.

13. Rosemary and Lavender Glycerin Soap

Ingredients:

-1 ½ teaspoon essential oil (Lavender)

- 3 cups of soap base (Glycerin)

- 1 ½ teaspoon of essential oil (Rosemary oil)

- ¼ cup of rosemary and lavender flowers (boiled in the water like herbal tea)

- 1 teaspoon of dried rosemary

Direction to prepare:

Take the glycerin soap base and melt it down in the microwave or you can use a double boiler but keep it on low flame. Let the soap melt down for 3 -5 minutes without stirring it. On the other hand take distilled water in a bowl and add in it the dried rosemary and lavender flowers and let them boil for 5 10minutes. Now pick the flowers out of the water and place them on the tissue paper. Once the glycerin soap base get melted, add in the essential oil, rosemary and lavender flowers placed on the tissue paper. Mix all the ingredients together. If you want your soap to be colored then you can use any color. Add the dye colorant in the mixture and stir it carefully.

Now take the mold, best is to take the mold of any flower shape of starfish shape to give it a beautiful and harming look. Grease it with vegetable or any oil. Now pour in it the mixture carefully. Let it set down for some minutes. Spray it with rubbing alcohol to avoid bubble formation. Place the mold in airy and cold place for 3 -4 hours. Once the soap get cooled down completely, unmold it carefully. You can cut it into small bars and can use it completely too.

If you want your soap to last longer than it is better to keep it in airy place for 3 weeks at least. Your patience will be worth as your soap will provide you refreshing bath for longer. You can even store it by properly wrapping it into plastic paper. It is the best gift you can give your family and friends.

Tips for Making Glycerin Soap

-Never store the soap in the place which is too cold or hot.

- Do not let one layer to get hard completely, Just little bit cooler (forming a thin layer) is enough and always spray the alcohol to avoid bubbles and it will also help the both layers to stick together well.

- Avoid to make soaps in humid weather, as it can interfere the setting process of the soap.

- Do not move the mold while soap is set for settling down as it can create cracks on the surface of the soap, if you face this situation, then immediately spray with rubbing alcohol as it will help relieve the cracks or wrinkles formed on the surface.

- If you wish your soap to settle down fast, then keep it in refrigerator for some time.

- Although the soap dry out mostly recommended in many recipes is few hours, but if you want your soap to last longer than always let your soap to dry out for 3 weeks once unmolded.

- Do not forget to spray rubbing alcohol before letting your soap to cool down to avoid bubble formation.

Conclusion

Homemade soap is not just the best way to utilize your free time into a productive hobby, but it can also make you start a little business at home and earn money, moreover you can prepare gift for your family and friends by customizing your soap according to your loved ones and surprise them on Christmas, Easter and birthday with these amazing homemade soaps.

You can indulge your kids in this healthy activity to use their energies in something productive and creative. It is the best way to get healthy soaps with the best natural ingredients to protect your skin from harsh chemicals which otherwise added in the soap available in the market. You can prepare many soaps at once and can use them over the period of a year or more. The best part is that you can customize the shape, color and fragrance of these soaps according to your own choice and enjoy the refreshing bath each and every time.

Thank You Page

I want to personally thank you for reading my book. I hope you found information in this book useful and I would be very grateful if you could leave your honest review about this book. I certainly want to thank you in advance for doing this.

www.ingramcontent.com/pod-product-compliance
Lightning Source LLC
La Vergne TN
LVHW021945060526
838200LV00042B/1928